T0083917

John Thompson's
SCALE-SPELLER

A Music Writing Book

Covering

All Major and Minor Scales and Key Signatures

and

Complete Table of Intervals

Exclusively Distributed By

WILLIS MUSIC

HAL•LEONARD®
CORPORATION
7777 W. BLUEMOUND RD. P.O. BOX 13819
MILWAUKEE, WISCONSIN 53213

Copyright, MCMXLVII, by the Willis Music Co.
International Copyright Secured

Printed in U.S.A.

CONTENTS

HALF STEPS and WHOLE STEPS............ 5

Naming WHOLE STEPS and HALF STEPS 6

Writing HALF STEPS and WHOLE STEPS 7

TETRACHORDS..................... 8

Writing TETRACHORDS................ 9

THE MAJOR SCALE................. 10

OVERLAPPING TETRACHORDS............ 11

Writing MAJOR SCALES............... 12

MINOR SCALES.................... 13

Writing HARMONIC MINOR SCALES........ 14

The MELODIC MINOR SCALE............. 15

Writing MELODIC MINOR SCALES.......... 16

CHROMATIC SCALES................. 18

INTERVALS...................... 19

Naming and Writing INTERVALS............ 20

DIATONIC INTERVALS................. 21

Writing MAJOR and PERFECT INTERVALS.. 22

CHROMATIC INTERVALS................ 23

DIMINISHED INTERVALS................ 24

AUGMENTED INTERVALS............... 25

Writing ALL INTERVALS................ 26

INVERSION OF INTERVALS.............. 28

SCALE FINGERING CHART............... 29

FOREWORD

When pupils can *write* the Scales correctly it is proof that they are really understood.

Many students have but a hazy idea of Intervals and Scales.

Some pianists *play* the Scales more or less by rote—since they are all the same pattern—but have limited knowledge of their *structure*.

The importance of really knowing scale construction is obvious, as it leads to a knowledge of chords later on.

For this reason it has been deemed wise to include the study and writing of Intervals thus preparing the pupil for John Thompson's CHORD SPELLER which should follow upon mastery of this book.

Scales should first be written with Accidentals, thus compelling the pupil to measure each step and half-step. Later, provision has also been made for writing the Signatures.

Only the Harmonic and Melodic Minor Scales are required to be written since the Natural Form of the minor is more or less theoretical and rarely encountered in actual piano playing.

Spelling in Music is just as important as spelling in the study of a Language—and can best be accomplished in a Writing Book.

J. T.

HALF STEPS

A HALF-STEP is the distance between any Key and the NEXT nearest Key.

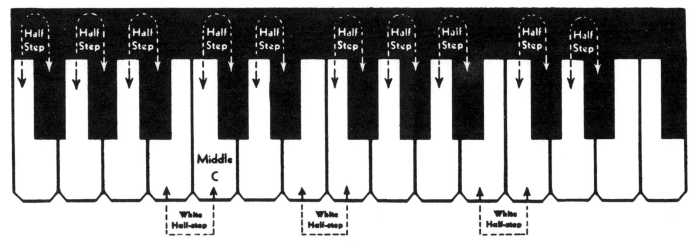

Most HALF-STEPS lie between a White Key and a Black Key.

There are however, two WHITE HALF-STEPS—one between B and C and the other between E and F. Study them on this chart and locate them on your piano keyboard until they can be quickly recognized.

WHOLE STEPS

A WHOLE STEP is twice the distance of a half-step. Therefore, there will always be ONE KEY—either BLACK or WHITE lying between.

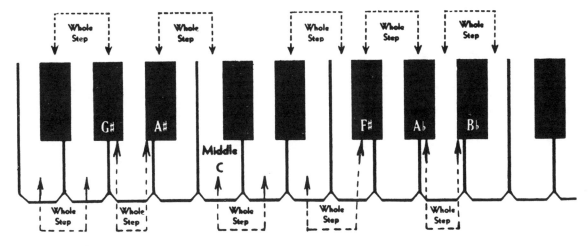

NAMING HALF STEPS and WHOLE STEPS

Mark Half-Steps with H and Whole Steps with W.

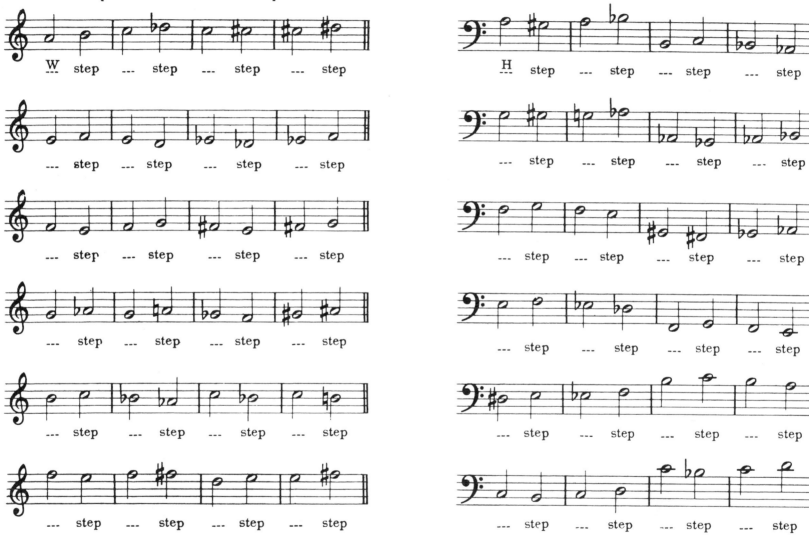

Copyright, *MCMXLVII,* by *The Willis Music Co.*
International Copyright Secured
Printed in U. S. A.

Write a Half-Step UPWARD from each of the notes shown below.

Write a Half-Step DOWNWARD from each of the notes shown below.

Write a Whole-Step UPWARD from the following.

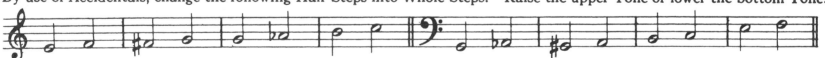

Write a Whole-Step DOWNWARD from the following.

By use of Accidentals, change the following Half-Steps into Whole-Steps.   Raise the upper Tone or lower the bottom Tone.

By use of Accidentals, change the following Whole-Steps into Half-Steps.   Lower the upper Tone or raise the lower Tone.

W.M.Co. 6584

TETRACHORDS

TETRACHORD (pronounced *Tet-ra-chord*) is a Greek name given to a group of four tones progressing in alphabetical order. The modern major TETRACHORD consists of *two whole-steps* and *one half-step* in the following order.

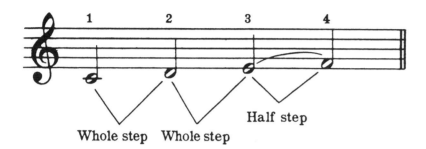

From 1 to 2 is a Whole Step.
From 2 to 3 is a Whole Step.
From 3 to 4 is a Half-Step.

TETRACHORDS may begin on any key by making use of the proper Accidentals necessary to preserve the pattern of *Two Whole-steps* and *One Half-step*.

ANALYSING TETRACHORDS

In the following Examples. mark all Whole-Steps with W and all Half-Steps with H.

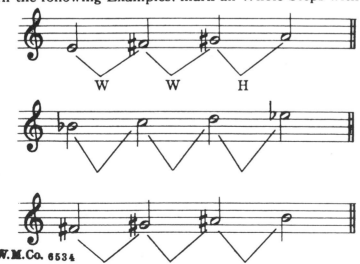

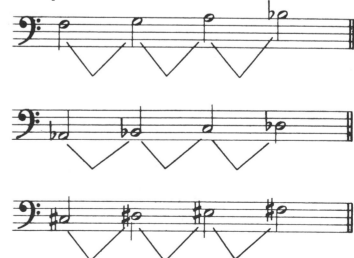

W.M.Co. 6534

WRITING TETRACHORDS

Write TETRACHORDS (ascending) in the following examples, beginning on the printed note.
Use the necessary ACCIDENTALS to preserve the pattern of TWO WHOLE STEPS AND ONE HALF STEP.

Mark each Half-Step with a curved line thus:

THE MAJOR SCALE

A SCALE is a succession of eight tones bearing letter-names in alphabetical order, the last tone having the same letter-name as the first. The figures 1, 2, 3, 4, 5, 6, 7, 8 are called the degrees of the scale.

A MAJOR SCALE is a succession of WHOLE steps and HALF steps.
The half steps occur between 3 and 4 and between 7 and 8 as follows:

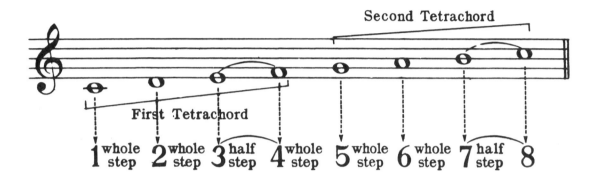

The above chart shows how a MAJOR SCALE is composed of TWO TETRACHORDS, each tetrachord *separated by a Whole step.*

ANALYSING THE SCALES

In the following Scales mark the Tetrachords with brackets.
Use a curved line to indicate the Half-Steps.

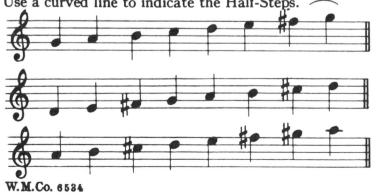

W.M.Co. 6534

OVERLAPPING TETRACHORDS

Each time a new Tetrachord is added, a new scale is formed.

In the example below note how the *upper* Tetrachord of one scale becomes the *lower* Tetrachord of the following scale.

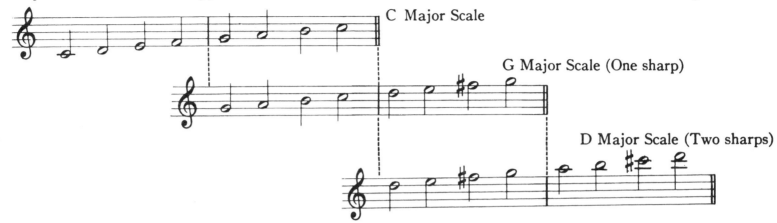

This *overlapping* of Tetrachords leads naturally through the Circle of Keys and finally returns to the Key of C major as shown in the chart below.

THE CIRCLE OF MAJOR KEYS

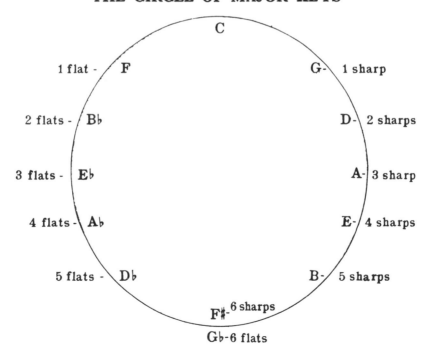

WRITING THE MAJOR SCALES

Write the Major Scales as indicated below *using Accidentals* as needed to form the Tetrachords.

After each scale is written, write its signature.

Mark the half-steps in the scales with a curved line.

How the sharps are placed

How the flats are placed

MINOR SCALES

The TONIC or KEY-NOTE of each Minor Scale is located upon the *Sixth Degree* of its Relative Major Scale.

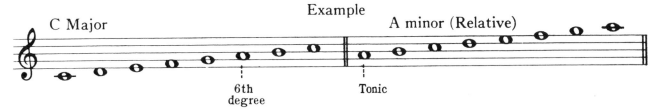

It will be seen that, except for a slight re-arrangement, the tones in the Minor Scale are exactly the same as those of **its** Relative Major.

This is known as the ANCIENT or NATURAL form of the Minor scale.

Our present Harmonic system requires however, a slight alteration in this form of the scale. This is done by *raising its seventh degree* one half-step.

The scale is then known as the HARMONIC MINOR SCALE.

THE HARMONIC MINOR SCALE

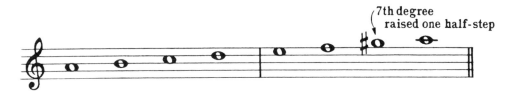

MINOR KEY SIGNATURES

All minor keys take their signatures from their Relative majors.

In other words, every signature stands for one of two keys. Either the major key—as already learned—or the Relative Minor key.

Examples

G major	F major	D major	B♭ major
or	or	or	or
E minor	D minor	B minor	G minor

WRITING HARMONIC MINOR SCALES

Write Harmonic Minor Scales according to the signatures given.
After each scale is written write the *name* of its Relative Major.

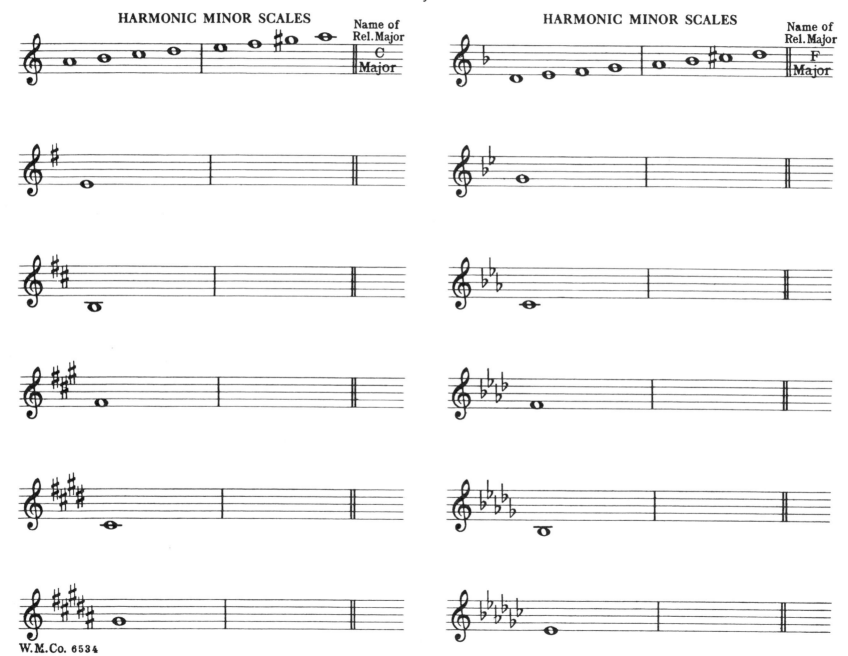

THE MELODIC MINOR SCALE

Another form of the Minor Scale is known as the MELODIC MINOR.

In the MELODIC MINOR form both the *sixth* and *seventh* degrees are raised as the scale ascends but *return to normal position* as the scale descends.   In other words, the Melodic Minor scale descends in the same form as the Natural Minor, described on page 12.

Example

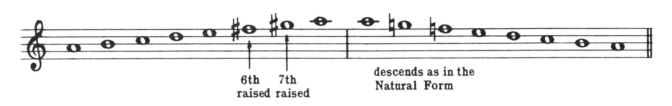

6th   7th
raised raised

descends as in the
Natural Form

THE THREE MINOR FORMS

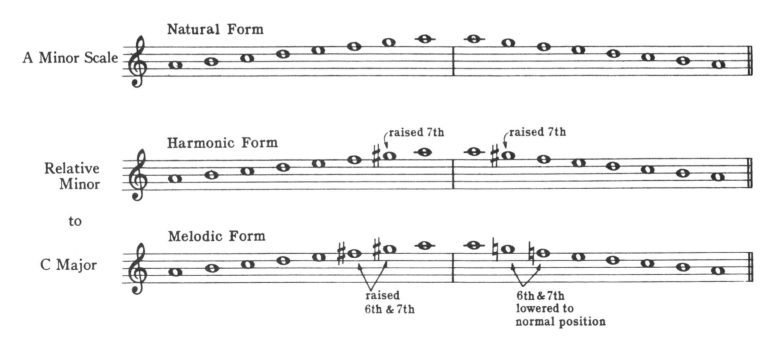

A Minor Scale — Natural Form

Relative
Minor — Harmonic Form — raised 7th   raised 7th

to

C Major — Melodic Form — raised 6th & 7th   6th & 7th lowered to normal position

W.M.Co. 6584

WRITING MELODIC MINOR SCALES

Write the Melodic Minor Scales ascending and descending.
Remember to raise the 6th and 7th degrees as the scale ascends and to lower them to normal as the scale descends.

Be sure to begin on the correct notes.

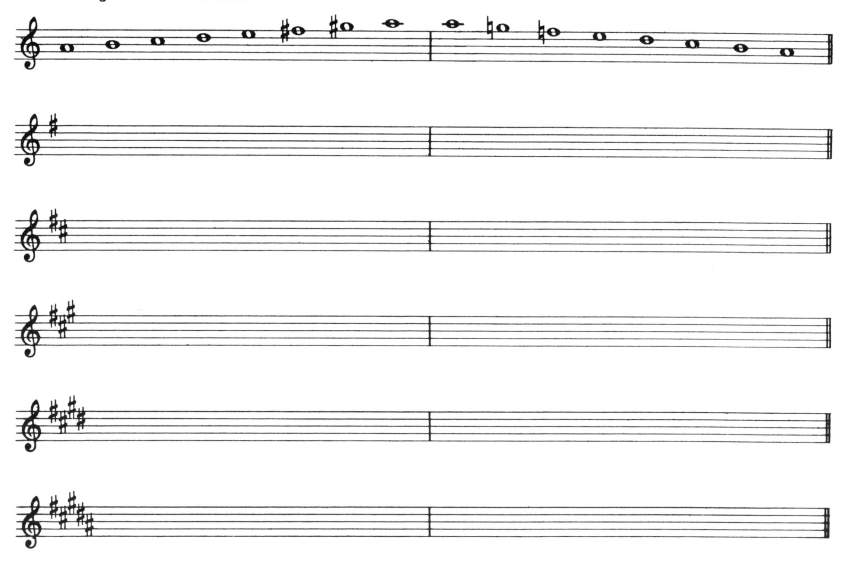

MELODIC MINOR SCALES

(Continued)

W.M.Co. 6534

CHROMATIC SCALES

A CHROMATIC SCALE is one which ascends or descends in half-steps.

Example

Chromatic tones are *raised* as the scale ascends and *lowered* as the scale descends.

Make Chromatic Scales of the following by use of the proper Accidentals.
Use the sharp or natural sign to *raise* the notes.
Use the flat or natural sign to *lower* the notes.

INTERVALS

An INTERVAL is the distance between two tones.

Intervals are measured in three ways.

1.—UPWARDS—Always count upward from the lower note.

2.—By the NUMBER OF NAMES OF NOTES they contain.—Count all letter-names lying between the lower and upper notes.

3.—INCLUSIVELY—Both outside notes are included in the counting.

The following examples show how easily INTERVALS can be measured.

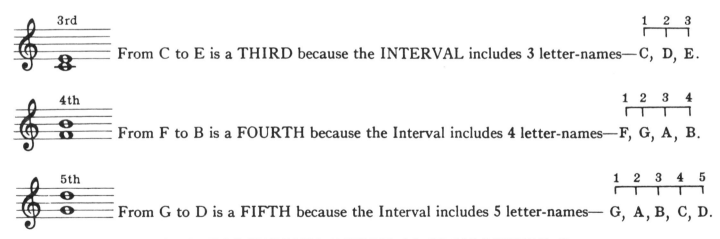

From C to E is a THIRD because the INTERVAL includes 3 letter-names—C, D, E.

From F to B is a FOURTH because the Interval includes 4 letter-names—F, G, A, B.

From G to D is a FIFTH because the Interval includes 5 letter-names— G, A, B, C, D.

SHOWING VARIOUS INTERVALS FROM MIDDLE C

NAMING and WRITING INTERVALS

Indicate the Intervals below by figures.

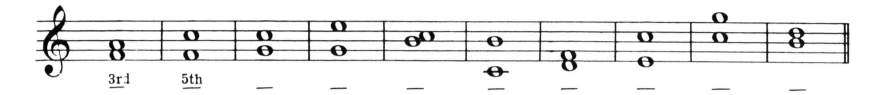

3rd   5th   —   —   —   —   —   —   —   —

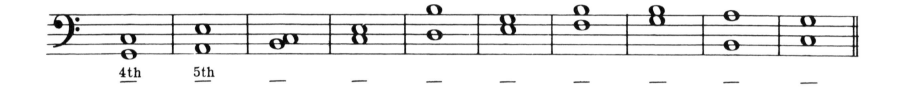

4th   5th   —   —   —   —   —   —   —   —

Fill in the *upper* notes to complete the following Intervals.

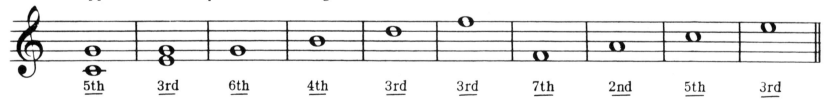

5th   3rd   6th   4th   3rd   3rd   7th   2nd   5th   3rd

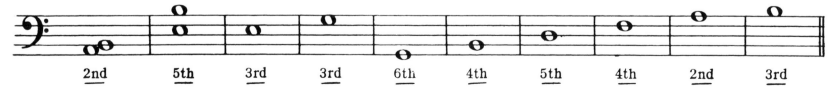

2nd   5th   3rd   3rd   6th   4th   5th   4th   2nd   3rd

W.M.Co. 6534

DIATONIC (or NATURAL) Intervals are those in which the upper tone *belongs to the major scale* of the lower tone. They are divided into two classes—PERFECT and MAJOR.—As shown below.

| *Perfect* | Major | Major | *Perfect* | *Perfect* | Major | Major | *Perfect* |
| Prime | Second | Third | *Fourth* | *Fifth* | Sixth | Seventh | *Octave* |

It will be seen that PRIMES, FOURTHS, FIFTHS and OCTAVES are called PERFECT. SECONDS, THIRDS, SIXTHS and SEVENTHS are called MAJOR.

NAMING DIATONIC INTERVALS

Mark Perfect Intervals P 1 — P 4 — P 5 — P 8 etc.
Mark Major Intervals M 2 — M 3 — M 6 — M 7 etc.

W.M.Co. 6534

WRITING MAJOR and PERFECT INTERVALS
in all KEYS

Write the *upper notes* needed to complete the Intervals indicated below.
Be sure to use the proper Accidentals.

Chromatic Intervals are those in which the upper tone does *not* belong to the major scale (of the lower tone).

There are three classes of Chromatic Intervals, namely, MINOR, DIMINISHED and AUGMENTED.

MINOR INTERVALS

A *minor* interval is formed *only* from a *major*, by lowering the upper degree a half-tone.

Example

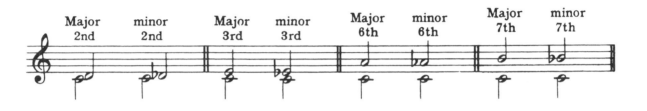

Reduce the following Major intervals to Minor by lowering the *upper* tone.   (DO NOT CHANGE THE LETTER-NAME).

To lower a note already flatted, use the double-flat sign—♭♭.

DIMINISHED INTERVALS

A DIMINISHED Interval is formed from a *minor* or *perfect* interval by lowering the upper degree a half-tone.

Example

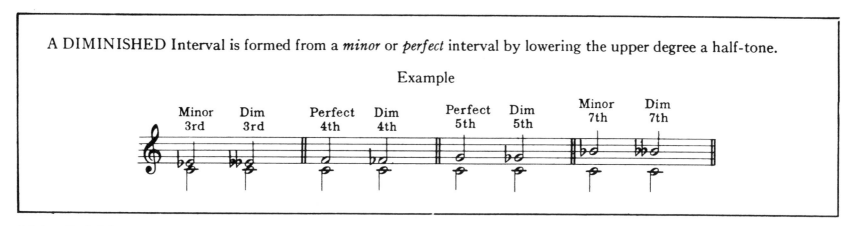

Make diminished intervals of the following, some of which are perfect and some are minor intervals.
Lower the *upper* tones but do *not* change the letter-names.

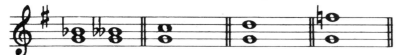

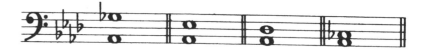

AUGMENTED INTERVALS

An AUGMENTED INTERVAL is formed from a *Major* or *Perfect* Interval by raising the upper tone one half-step.

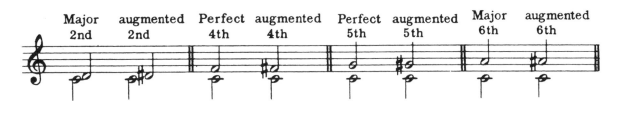

Make Augmented Intervals of the following by raising the upper tones.

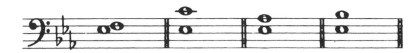

To raise a tone already sharped, use the double-sharp sign— ✕

WRITING ALL THE INTERVALS

To raise a note already sharped use the double sharp sign,— ✗

W.M.Co. 6534

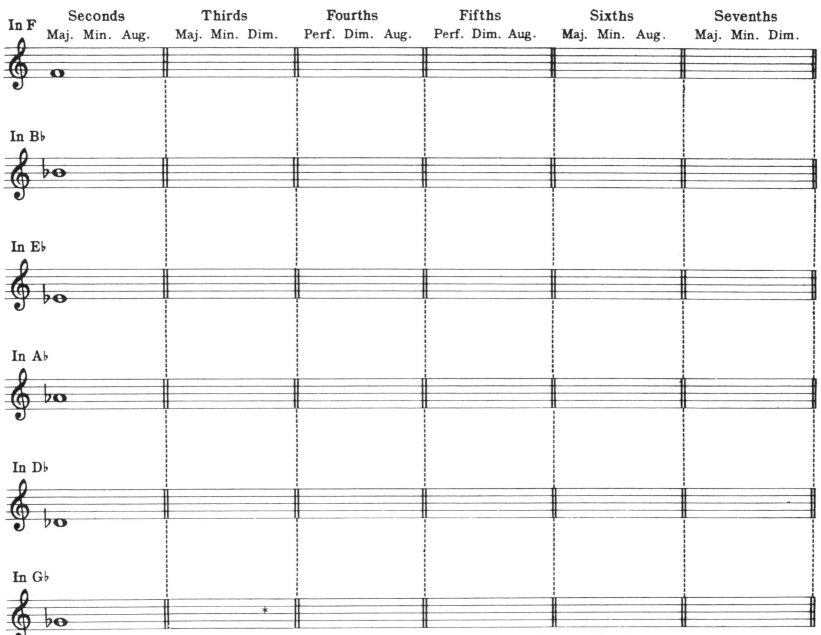

*The interval of a diminished third is theoretically possible by using a B triple flat, but this interval is extremely rare in music.

To lower a note already flatted use the double-flat sign— ♭♭

INVERSION OF INTERVALS

An INVERTED INTERVAL, as its name suggests, is one which has been reversed—the original lower tone now appearing on top.

When inverted most intervals reverse their classification also.
Only the Perfect intervals remain Perfect as will be seen in the examples below.

A Major interval becomes Minor . . . .   Major Third becomes a Minor Sixth.

A Minor interval becomes Major . . . .   Minor Sixth becomes a Major Third.

A Diminished Interval becomes Augmented . . . .   Diminished Seventh becomes an Augmented Second.

An Augmented interval becomes Diminished . .   Augmented Fifth becomes a Diminished Fourth.

A Perfect interval remains Perfect . . . .   *Perfect Fifth becomes a Perfect Fourth.*

Invert the Intervals below and name them before and after inversion.
Use M for Major—mi for minor—A for Augmented—D for Diminished—P for Perfect.

SCALE FINGERING CHART

FOR SCALES BEGINNING ON WHITE KEYS

MAJOR SCALES
C–G–D–A–E

Right Hand—The Thumb falls on the FIRST and FOURTH degrees of the scale.
(End with the 5th finger)

Left Hand — The Thumb falls on the FIRST and FIFTH degrees of the scale.
(Begin with the 5th finger)

There are two exceptions to the above rules—the scales of B major and F major. They are fingered as follows:

B MAJOR—Begin with the 4th finger in the left hand.

F MAJOR—End with the 4th finger in the right hand

In the B and F scales, the thumbs of both hands *always play together* (except for the lower and upper notes of the scale).

MINOR SCALES

The WHITE KEY MINOR SCALES are fingered exactly the same as the WHITE KEY MAJOR SCALES (of the same letter-names).

FOR SCALES BEGINNING ON BLACK KEYS

MAJOR SCALES
Bb–Eb–Ab–Db

Right Hand—4th finger on Bb (or A♯)
Left Hand —4th finger on the 4th degree of the scale.
(Begin with 3rd finger).

Gb (or F♯) is the only exception to the above rules. To finger this scale see that the *Thumbs play together on the White Keys.* (There are only two white keys in the scale).

MINOR SCALES

Bb Minor } Thumbs play together on the *first two* White
Eb Minor } Keys of each scale.

————

Ab (or G♯) Minor—Fingered exactly the same as Ab (or G♯) Major.

————

C♯ Minor } R.H.—4th finger falls on the second degree of each scale.

F♯ Minor } L.H.—4th finger falls on F♯ in each scale.

W.M.Co. 6534